GW00632239

# Back to the Sea

## An introduction to Peter Frederick Anson and his life in the east coast of Scotland.

*Peter Anson at Macduff Harbour.*
*(Courtesy Raymond Jaconelli, Abbot, Nunraw Abbey).*

*Peter Anson at the door of Harbour Head, No. 2 Low Shore, Macduff.*
*(Courtesy Raymond Jaconelli, Abbot, Nunraw Abbey).*

# Back to the Sea

An introduction to Peter Frederick Anson
and his life in the east coast of Scotland.

## By
## Stanley Bruce
## and
## Tina Harris

Published by
BARD BOOKS
On behalf of the
Banffshire Maritime & Heritage Association

♦ Back to the Sea ♦

**First Edition.**

ISBN 978-1-907234-00-2

**This edition published in 2009 by Bard Books.**

**All proceeds from the sale of this book will be donated to the
Banffshire Maritime & Heritage Association.
Registered Charity Number SCO40505.**

*Printed by Cooper Printers, Fraserburgh.*

## Contents      Page

*Peter Anson (1889 to 1975).*

## Introduction

'Back to the Sea' is a very fitting title for a book about Peter Frederick Anson who loved the sea so much, it was clearly the most enjoyable part of his life. Peter was born in Southsea, Portsmouth in 1889, and his real name was Frederick Charles Anson. He took the name of Peter in 1924 after the Apostle Peter the fisherman, when he took the brown scapular. In this book we refer to him as Peter Anson, the name he chose for himself. Peter Anson initially wrote books about religion, but his interest in the sea inspired many books about fishermen and the sea. Peter published a total of forty-seven books, and illustrated four others during his lifetime. During his time in the north east of Scotland he published thirty-one books. In 2005, Michael Yelton of the Anglo-Catholic History Society wrote 'Peter Anson: Monk, Writer and Artist' – this book covers the religious aspect of Peter's life, but mentions very little about his life in Scotland or his writing about fishing and the fishing communities. This book serves to fill this gap.

Some local people have told me that Peter was a very modest man, Valerie Smith told me that when Peter lived in Montrose her mother invited him to dinner, and that Peter insisted he would only come if there wasn't any other folk there, other than her, her mother, her brother, and Jack Smith. However in one of his books he wrote that his father destroyed a lot of his family documents because he thought Peter would find a way to publish them, and his father didn't want that.

*Peter Anson – The Caravan Pilgrim. (1938).*

There seems to have been two sides to Peter, one where he would often like time by himself and some privacy, and another where he loved meeting people, talking about their lives, taking an interest and learning about them. So he was clearly a modest man, but not a shy man, a shy man could never have achieved what he did, travelling all over the world meeting strangers and quickly making friends.

This book is intended to introduce you to Peter, his life in the north east of Scotland, and perhaps most importantly, his lifetime achievements. All so you can understand why we feel the erection of a sculpture to his memory in Macduff is so appropriate.

Peter Anson was a very religious man, and his first love was God, but it is also clear that he had a great love of the sea, and no greater a tribute could he have, except perhaps when he was honoured by the Pope, when in 1930 a Buckie fisherman said "Peter has the sea in his blood".

Peter experienced life to the full, he sailed with the fishermen, he learnt their methods, he travelled all along the British coastline and further afield. Peter left a legacy which includes paintings or drawings of virtually every fishing port throughout the UK from Stornoway to Hastings; his drawings depict fishing boats and harbour scenes. Many of his 1920's drawings valuably show the fishing methods of the time. In his later years he drew water-colour paintings of the Scottish fishing ports many of which are now in the care of the Moray Council. In the 1930's he even perhaps eccentrically travelled in a horse drawn gypsy caravan as told in his book titled 'The Caravan Pilgrim' published in 1938. Peter was truly an exceptional man.

*Stanley A. Bruce,*
*BSc, I.Eng. MIMarEST.*
*Chairman, Banffshire Maritime & Heritage Association.*

*Drawing titled 'Packing white fish on a trawler' by Peter Anson.*

**Authors Note**

It is indeed a humbling experience to be involved in gathering together the key facts of Peter Anson's time in the north east of Scotland. It was by chance that I discovered the scale of his local involvement, when I visited Portsoy in 2002. Although I share his faith and interest, I had not fully appreciated that I am now resident less than a mile from the site of Harbour Head his former Macduff home.

I moved to Macduff because, like Peter, I have the sea in my blood. What better place to be than overlooking the Moray Firth to the hills of the north; to hear the waves lapping on Low Shore, and to venture out on a boat whenever.

Peter Anson has not only left a lasting legacy to Macduff and the north east coast of Scotland, but also to the world through the ongoing work of the Apostleship of the Sea, which is now recognised as the frontline service for the care of seafarers.

I hope this booklet will draw together those who wish to remember Peter Anson and his extensive legacy to the fishing industry, and introduce him to many others.

*Tina Harris, B.Ed.,*
*Committee member,*
*Banffshire Maritime & Heritage Association.*

**Note to the Title**

In the 1920's Peter wrote a pamphlet titled "The Scottish Fisheries – are they doomed?" which found favour in several leading newspapers of the time. His blue-covered pamphlet ended with the words "We need a new slogan – **Back to the Sea**".

*Peter Anson.*

## Early Years

Frederick Charles Anson (He changed his name in 1924 to Peter) was born on 22nd August 1889 at 32 South Parade, Southsea, Portsmouth, England. He was the eldest child of four to Charles Eustace Anson (1858 to 1940) who rose to the position of Rear-Admiral and Maria Evelyn Ross (c1863 to 1905). Peter had two sisters Edith (b.1893), and Rachel (b.1894), and a brother Horatio (b.1903). Peter logs his first clear vision

*Rear-Admiral Charles Anson. Peter's father.*

of a ship as a "white painted, three masted ship".
However it was from Mrs Evelyn Anson his mother, that the real roots of the sea and Scotland came. She, although born on the Isle of Mull had roots from Rossie Castle, near Montrose. She took Peter many times to see the Scottish herring boats berth in the ports of Southern England. And so the seeds were sown. Peter claims he was always dressed in a sailor suit (a reduced version of a naval seaman's uniform) until the age of about ten. Without a doubt, Peter Anson was born with the sea in his blood. Both sides of his family had close ties with the sea, and as a child from the age of six years he began sketching boats with great detail and accuracy. This obsession for detail is evident in his later work, and he stated that his mission was:

"To produce a realistic record which could be understood by ordinary folk".

In the summer of 1898 a young red-haired Peter attended 'Little Appley' a small preparatory School in Ryde, Isle of Wight. Peter states that he was a "Tiresome and difficult pupil", and his end of term reports stated he was "Frivolous and volatile". In 1902 he attended Wixenford boarding school, Wokingham (Founded in 1892) which at the time was one of the most expensive preparatory schools in England. His fees were paid for out of a captain's pay, which shows how important Peter's schooling was to his father Charles Anson. Peter wrote in one of his books that he liked it a Wixenford School, and Peter left the school in 1904 just before his 15th birthday.

## Architectural Association School, London

Peter enrolled at the Architectural College in Tufton Street, Westminster, London in 1908. He studied there for two years before deciding it wasn't for him. Peter didn't attend for the third year of the course, so never left with any qualifications. During his time at the college Peter joined the College Camera and Sketching Club, and from 30th July to 10th August 1909 travelled from Le Harve to Rouen in France. Both of these drawings on this page clearly show his name as 'F.C. Anson'. The drawing of St George's in France was taken from the Architectural Association Journal Vol. XXIV, No. 272 dated October 1909.

*St George's Boscherville, France, by F.C.A. 1909.*

SCHOOL OF ARCHITECTURE—*continued.*]

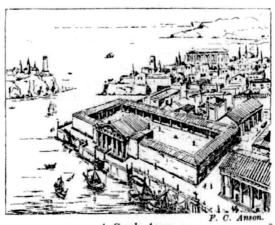

*A Greek Agora taken from the Architectural Association Journal Vol. XXV, No. 276, by F. C. Anson dated February 1910.*

## Religion

In 1910 Peter joined the Anglican Benedictine community on Caldey Island and became a monk. He was received into the Roman Catholic Church in 1913.

"I might be giving up the world", he wrote, "But this would not involve me giving up the sea...it would be too much to ask".

He then took the name Richard, his name at birth being Frederick Charles Anson. In 1924 after joining a Franciscan Order in Italy, he took the name of Peter, after the Apostle Peter, who was a fisherman. It was the name Peter which adorned all of his forty-seven books, and thousands of paintings and drawings.

Peter Anson devoted his life to his interest in the sea, fishing, and the Catholic Church. His personal faith and his love for the sea were his true inspiration.

Peter is known to have visited Our Lady of Mount Carmel Church in Sandyhill Road, Banff; and using his architectural knowledge, also advised on the colour schemes for the redecoration of the Church of the Annunciation in Portsoy (now closed), although there is little in the diocesan archive to support this, or indeed to suggest he worshipped regularly in either church.

We should indeed not forget that for six years there was a Roman Catholic place of worship in the little fisherman's cottage 'Harbour Head' No 2 Low Shore, beside Macduff Harbour where Peter Anson had made his home. The small attic chapel Peter named the 'Chapel of our Lady of the Ships and St Peter the Fisherman'. Macduff was therefore the only port in Scotland with a Catholic chapel set aside specifically for mariners.

## Local Memories

A local Macduff man recalled that Peter had a bit of a stutter, and when he got excited or angry he could end up not being able to speak at all. This speech impediment and his health problems are probably the reason why Peter never excelled in the Church.

*Macduff Harbour by Peter Anson.*
*Taken from 'Fishermen and Fishing Ways' published 1932.*

## Apostleship of the Sea

Peter Anson was a co-founder of the Apostleship of the Sea (AOS) in 1921. This society is now the frontline service for the spiritual, social and material welfare of Catholic seafarers, known affectionately in over 100 countries throughout the world as "Stella Maris". The AOS now touches the lives of 100 million seafarers each year. The Apostleship of the Sea badge, originally designed by Peter, may be worn by all members. This emblem although now slightly modified, shows an anchor, a lifebelt, and a heart at its centre, and is the official badge of the AOS.

*Apostleship of the Sea emblem.*

*Oratory of our Lady of the Ships, Harbour Head, Macduff.*
*(Photographer unknown – 1940's).*

Peter's Oratory in the attic of Harbour Head, Macduff had a frontal that was of green sail cloth edged with rope, and a cover of tanned sail cloth. The model boats in the photograph were made by young Campbell Cowie (1922 to 1941) of Macduff. On the left is a statue of the Virgin Mary in a small boat, coincidently the Virgin Mary is the emblem of Banff.

*Banff Mercat Cross & Virgin Mary. (S. Bruce).*

*Baiting the lines by Peter Anson.*
*Taken from 'Fishermen and Fishing Ways' published in 1932.*

www.apostleshipofthesea.org.uk

14

**Peter Anson the Artist**

Peter drew in his early years, but it wasn't until 1919 that his drawing actually came to fruition when he illustrated a book for Sir D. Hunter-Blair titled 'Medley of Memories: 50 years' Recollection of a Benedictine Monk'. Peter's time at the Architectural Association School in London (1908 to 1910) certainly influenced his drawings, of which were first-rate. In 1936 Peter was a founder member of the Society of Marine Artists. This Society was renamed the 'Royal Society of Marine Artists' in 1966. His skill in drawing, particularly the fine detail is also evident in his drawings of fishing boats and fishermen.

*Peter Anson - drawing. (Courtesy J. Kelly Editor of The Universe newspaper).*

The most wonderful description of Peter was by a Buckie fisherman who said "Peter's the maist winnerfu' mannie ah ever met - well-kent in scores o' ports - a man wi' the sea in's bleed, a skeely drawer o' boats an' haibers an' fisher fowk, a vreeter o' buiks, a capital sailor, an' 'a chiel.... He's a byordinar mannie!" Translated this means: Peter is the most wonderful man I ever met – well known in scores of ports – a man with the sea in his blood, a skilful drawer of boats and harbours and fisher folk, a writer of books, a capital sailor and a good man. He's an extra-ordinary man!

From 1929 to 1936 Peter was truly a 'Roving Recluse' and travelled all over Europe and further, making drawings of churches and abbeys for 'The Universe' newspaper (founded in 1860), which were reproduced each week in the paper. He became known as the 'Pilgrim Artist' and had over 800 drawings published. During this period he travelled to France, Italy, Belgium, Holland, Denmark, Norway, Sweden, Palestine, Egypt, Ireland, and of course England, Scotland, and Wales.

His drawings provide a very valuable record of many harbours and fishing vessels. Peter's studies at the Architectural Association School in London, gives rise to his distinctive style. Many of Peter's drawings and paintings of fishing boats have been gifted to the National Maritime Museum in London, and in 1973 he presented four hundred of his water-colours to newly established Buckie Maritime Museum. These are now in the care of the Moray Council. Copyright of his work he bequeathed to the Abbot of Nunraw Abbey.

## Peter Anson the Writer

Peter wrote forty-seven books, eleven of which have a maritime theme relating to the north east of Scotland.

Many renowned authors and artists have commented on Peter's work, which can be summed up by his good friend Neil M. Gunn (1891 to 1973) author of twenty novels including the much acclaimed book 'The Silver Darlings' (1941), who commented in his introduction to Peter's book 'Life on Low Shore' published in 1969,

"He brought the sea with him".

Neil Gunn also wrote the foreword of Peter's book 'The Scottish Fisheries – are they doomed' in 1939. It is said that it was Peter who pushed Neil Gunn to write 'The Silver Darlings', and perhaps it would never have been written if he hadn't.

Peter knew in detail every rock, bay, jetty, and harbour on the Moray Firth coast and beyond; and portrayed them on paper with the patience of a saint.

In 1966 Peter was created a Knight of the Order of St Gregory by Pope Paul VI, in recognition of his prolific literary achievements.

Since Peter's death a number of his books have been republished, including his best-seller 'How to Draw Ships' first published in 1941.

*Peter Anson, 1940's.*
*(Photo - Frank Ritchie).*

**Life in NE Scotland**

Peter made lifelong friends among the fishing communities from Nairn to Arbroath, and further, but it was in Macduff that he settled for the longest. He visited the Moray Firth fishing communities in the 1920's, and many of his drawings and paintings date from this time, however it was 1936 before he decided to make a home there. Peter did a lot of his drawings from photographs and below we have a good example, this 1921 scene at Buckie Harbour was drawn by Peter while at Caldey Abbey fifty-two years later in 1973.

SELLING FISH AT BUCKIE. 1921.    P.F.ANSON 1973.

*Selling fish at Buckie 1921, by Peter Anson 1973.*

**Portsoy**

In May 1936 Peter moved to his first home on the Moray Firth, which was a fisherman's cottage in Portsoy.

**Banff**

In December 1936 Peter moved into two unfurnished rooms at Braeheads in Banff. Braeheads is the row of houses shown in Peter's drawing below in the top right corner. From here Peter would have had a good view of Banff Harbour and across Banff Bay to Macduff. Peter lived here for two years, before moving to Harbour Head, No. 2 Low Shore, Macduff, in May 1938. On the 21st October 2008 the Banffshire Journal reported that 8 Braeheads, Banff from 1778 to 1792 was used as a secret Jacobite breakaway chapel. This was after St Andrew's Church in Banff was burned to the ground by Cumbernauld's Army in 1746 after the Battle of Culloden.

Braeheads

*Banff Harbour 1929 drawn by Peter Anson, taken from 'Fishing Boats and Fisher Folk on the East Coast of Scotland' published 1930.*

*Harbour Head, No. 2 Low Shore, Macduff. (Photo – Frank Ritchie).*

**Macduff**
Peter made his home in Macduff, at No. 2 Low Shore in May 1938. This was a small cottage affectionately known as 'Harbour Head', where Peter lived for fourteen years (1938 to 1952). This house was a typical fisherman's cottage built between 1800 and 1840. The cottage consisted of three rooms, and a lean-to scullery added in the early 1900's. In the corner of the kitchen there was a deep recess with a traditional built-in bed. Like other fishermen's cottages of this period it had small windows and a very small garden of which Peter referred to it as a 'Yardie'. Peter commented in his book 'Life on Low Shore' "...the windows were so small; I heard more than I saw". During the war years and beyond the house was open to all, and in this cottage Peter converted the loft into a chapel with a maritime theme.

"Few of our readers know of this centre, but there is a warm welcome at the door for every visitor; yet there is neither church nor resident priest in the burgh. I have gone back there many times and found every visit as thrilling as the first. No fewer than 5,000 visitors have been at the Centre in the last twelve months". Jack Smith, in the Catholic Herald, 1943.

Aelred Carlyle, former Abbot of Caldey, said of Harbour Head, in September 1948; "It looks like Peter and feels like Peter at his best." Aelred said Mass in what he described as "The quaintest chapel imaginable, with a strong smell of tar, old rope and canvas."

Sadly Harbour Head was demolished in 1974, and in its place now stands the Harbour Café, appropriately still providing refreshments to fishermen and visitors.

Whilst resident at Harbour Head, Peter bought in 1940 for £2.00 a fifteen foot long sail boat, which he named the 'Stella Maris', which means 'Star of the Sea'. While at Caldey Island Peter had sailed on a boat called 'Stella Maris', so he named his boat in memory of his times at Caldey. This boat was registered in his name under the Banff registration BF75. This is recorded in the Mariners' Almanac of 1941, and Peter proudly displayed his 'Certificate of Registration' on the lobby wall of Harbour Head. The boat was painted grey and had bright blue gunwales, and was sailed by Peter and youngsters of Macduff during the summer months. It was scrapped in 1949.

*BF75 'Stella Maris', Peter Anson in the middle and Campbell Cowie at the helm. (Courtesy Raymond Jaconelli, Abbot, Nunraw Abbey).*

An influential sailor George Smith, son of a Buckie steam drifter fisherman, and apprenticed to the Macduff boat building yard made a few alterations in the dipping lugsail of the 'Stella Maris', and after this, Peter says in his book Life on Low Shore (1969), "miracles began to be performed at sea, in the sense that BF75 moved through the water when there did not appear to be a breath of air."

"Life on Low Shore was never dull, what with writing books and painting pictures". Peter Anson 1944.

Peter's home at Harbour Head was often referred to as an 'open house' because it was always open to the crews of various classes of vessels that visited Macduff, but his home was much more than that, it was open to the youngsters of the town, who would go down and see Peter, and learn some of the trades of the sea, such as making knots, net-making and sailing. Peter found it strange that in a fishing orientated town that the boys didn't already know all of this nautical stuff. Those interested in art, learnt some of Peter's drawing and painting techniques. The most notable of all the boys who spent a lot of time with Peter was Campbell Cowie (1922 to 1941). He was born in Macduff, and at a young age had left to join the Navy, however once in the Navy he was diagnosed with a disease known as Acromegaly, and was discharged. This disease gave him large features, his hands were said to be huge. Despite this Peter states that Campbell was a very intelligent young lad who had won prizes at school. Peter dedicated his book Harbour Head to the memory of Campbell Cowie and nine pages of his book titled 'A Roving Recluse' (Published in 1946) is all about Campbell Cowie, indicating how fond he was of him. Peter also states that when he wrote his best-selling book 'How to Draw Ships' "The amazing success of this little book is largely due to Campbell". Campbell had proof-read several of Peter's books including 'How to Draw Ships' and never failed to detect Peter's mistakes in spelling and grammar. Campbell Cowie despite his large hands was an expert model-maker and built many model boats. Peter and Campbell visited Iona and when they returned to Macduff together they spent six weeks building a model of the monastic buildings. This fine model was later exhibited at the Royal Scottish Academy. When Campbell's mother died he went to live with Peter. Campbell Cowie is pictured at the helm of Peter's boat BF75 'Stella Maris' on page 20. Sadly due to his illness Campbell died aged only nineteen; and is he buried in Macduff Cemetery.

In 1945 Peter was commissioned to study Irish fisheries, and he also represented the Irish Government when a number of fishing boats were built for them in Banff. In 1946 he wrote a book titled 'The Sea Apostolate in Ireland'.

*How to Draw Ships by Peter Anson, published 1941.*

In his book, 'Fishing Boats and Fisher Folk on the East Coast of Scotland' (Published 1930), Peter has entered statistical tables based on data from 1881 to 1928. It is interesting to note that in an 1885 survey there were no less than 205 Fishermen and Boys, working out of Macduff on seventy boats, ranging in size from eighteen to over thirty feet. To add to the picture there were recorded 609 persons involved in the various fish processing, curing, vending and net making businesses in the town. Peter Anson comments in his book 'Fishing Boats and Fisher Folk on the East Coast of Scotland' (Published in 1930) that: "The rise of Macduff as an important fishing centre is comparatively recent".

The harbour, he claimed, also in 1930, was one of the best on the Moray Firth, and specialised in seine-net fishing during the spring months.

In one of Peter's introductions he dedicates his work to:

"all my fishermen friends on the east coast of Scotland".

Although his research traced the decline of the fishing industry throughout the early years of the last century, Peter sought to highlight the positive, and it is this that truly shows his faith in the fishers of the north east of Scotland.

In 1952 Peter sold his fisherman's cottage Harbour Head and left Macduff for the south of England. Seven months later – Peter returned to stay in Macduff, again he lived in a fisherman's cottage in Low Shore, sited to the east of Harbour Head. It is thought he regretted selling Harbour Head. (Both houses are now demolished).

Towards the end of the 1950's, the Banffshire Journal published a leading article aimed at women readers, about a "Mere man in Macduff, whose hospitality has extended to more than

*British Sea-Fishermen by Peter Anson, published in 1944.*

3,000 cups of tea, coffee, and cocoa a year since the beginning of 1948..."

The article goes on to explain that "Mr Anson (Whose 'galley' cannot stand up to the hospitality unlimited), has now secured the approval of the Food Control Committee in the manner of applying for a licence which will enable him to replenish his stores by way of trade..."

The scheme was approved, and building works commenced to enlarge the 'galley' to accommodate more customers. Peter's cottage in Low Shore remained a House of Hospitality until it was sold in 1958.

### Portsoy
After a spell in a cottage near Ramsgate Abbey, Peter returned to the Moray Firth, and in 1960 Peter lived at Park House B+B, Haywood Drive, Portsoy. In September 1960 he moved to Montrose.

***Portsoy Harbour by Peter Anson. Taken from 'Fishermen and Fishing Ways' published in 1932.***

**Montrose**

Peter moved from Portsoy to Montrose in September 1960. Here he lived with a good friend of his, Jack Smith. Jack Smith and Peter had a lot in common, and are known to have got on very well. Peter lived with Jack in a twelve-roomed house which Jack had inherited from his parents. Jack's house was known as 'The Song of the Sea'. Jack was a well-known figure in Montrose; he was a lay-preacher and a journalist, and latterly wrote a column for the *Montrose Review*. Jack was a seafarer during WW2, he sailed as a cook on the 'Lochside II' a cargo ship, which regularly carried beer from Newcastle. Jack also owned the local fishing boat the 'Mizpah'. Jack's house stood on the north bank of the harbour near where the RNLI lifeboat station stands today, the house has since been demolished.

Peter Anson had family roots in Montrose through his Scottish mother Maria Evelyn Ross (c1863 to 1905); Peter's great, great grandfather on his mother's side - Hercules Ross (1745 to 1816) built Rossie Castle c1795 which stood about one mile south of Montrose. It was designed by Architect Richard Crichton (c1771 to 1817) of Edinburgh. It was demolished around 1957.

*Rossie Castle, Montrose. (Now demolished).*

**Ferryden**
26th December 1961 Peter's good friend Jack Smith bought a large fisherman's cottage No. 17 William Street, Ferryden near Montrose, and Peter moved with him. In July 1962 Jack Smith got married to Helen Carnegie who owned an up-market ladies clothes shop in Montrose.

*No. 17 William Street, Ferryden. (S. Bruce).*

Peter then moved out of Jack's fisherman's cottage No. 17 William Street, Ferryden to an unfurnished attic in No 19 King Street, Ferryden, which was the home of Andrew Mearns the local pilot and skipper of the 'Angus Rose', and his wife Annie-May Mearns. From his attic bay window Peter had a great view of the harbour. Annie-May is said to have regularly complained about Peter tapping away on his old typewriter at 4.00am in the morning; a typical writer writing things down when they came to mind. No. 19 King Street, Ferryden is now owned by Mr George Peattie who knew Peter Anson well. Around fifteen-years after Peter's death Mr Peattie recalled that his teenage daughter Suzie said that one night there was a man in her bedroom; however she thought she must have been dreaming. When she gave a description of an old man dressed in black, wearing glasses, and a grey goat beard, he knew it was the ghost of Peter Anson back from the dead. He also recalled that Peter (as seen on the cover of this book) looked more like a fisherman with his reefer jacket and cap than many of the local fishermen did. Mr Peattie also stated that Peter didn't bother anybody; he simply got on with his business, and he never saw Peter preach religion to anyone.

In February 1963 Peter purchased No. 1 King Street, Ferryden, however he didn't move into the house until 1st May 1963. The current owner of the house stated that this house used to have two external staircases, and that local fishermen used to bait the lines in front of the house, and on occasions, presumably during bad weather, in Peter's living room. (See photograph on page 28).

*No. 19 King Street, Ferryden.*
*(S. Bruce).*

*1 to 5 King Street, Ferryden. (S. Bruce). No. 1 is the house at the rear.*

This photograph shows left Norrie West, and right Tom Nicol crew of
ME34 'Rosemary' and Peter Anson baiting lines inside Peter's house
No. 1 King Street, Ferryden.  Note the huge collection of books.
(Courtesy Raymond Jaconelli, Abbot, Nunraw Abbey).

**Last Years**

Failing health impelled Peter Anson to seek a mainland home, and early in 1975 he moved from the abbey at Caldey Island, and was accepted into what was to become his final resting place within the community of Nunraw Abbey (Sancta Maria Abbey), in East Lothian, the only Cistercian monastic community in Scotland.

*Peter Anson.*

Peter died 10th July 1975, in St. Raphael's Hospital in Edinburgh, and is buried in the private cemetery for deceased monks at Nunraw Abbey. Robert O'Brien of Caldey Abbey recalled that it was Peter's wish to be buried at sea, and that Peter was very disappointed that this couldn't be arranged.

*The private cemetery at Nunraw Abbey, East Lothian, the resting place for deceased monks. (Renata Edge).*

the Order of St. Gregory' in 1966, in recognition of his prolific literary and scholarly achievements.

The fishing boat ME34 'Rosemary' as shown in this water-colour painting by Peter was owned by Jimmy Patten of Ferryden whose tee-name was 'Skinum'. Skinum was well known to Peter Anson.

*ME34 MV 'Rosemary' berthed at Ferryden, painted by Peter Anson in 1971.*

**Caldey Island**

In 1969 Peter returned to the abbey at Caldey Island, where he had lived and returned to many times in his life. In his heart this is where he wanted to spend the rest of his life.

*Caldey Abbey by Peter Anson.*

Here he continued painting – mainly from photographs, and Robert O'Brien also at the abbey at the time recalled that Peter painted a water-colour every morning before breakfast, after breakfast he had his monastic duties to do. Also at this time he completed his book titled

'Fishing Boats and Fisher Folk on the East Coast of Scotland' which was published in 1971. Robert O'Brien of Caldey Abbey recalled that Peter had prostate cancer which was diagnosed late, and even after having an operation was forced to seek a mainland home. In 1975 although a dying man he moved to Nunraw Abbey in East Lothian which had its own infirmary.

*Arbroath Harbour painted by Peter Anson in 1974.*
*(Courtesy Graham and Anne Smith, Ferryden).*

## Anstruther

In April 1967 Peter was approached to take on the job of Collector / Curator at the new Scottish Fisheries Museum in Anstruther. Peter accepted the invitation immediately; however his appointment wasn't confirmed until 8th July 1967. Peter's time at the museum was however a short one, early in January 1968 he submitted his resignation because he was unhappy about his job description which was never clearly defined. Peter however donated some of his paintings to the museum.

*The Scottish Fisheries Museum, Anstruther. (S. Bruce).*

## Ferryden

Peter returned to Ferryden, near Montrose in January 1968. He resided at No. 3 King Street an upstairs flat, where he stayed until 1969. Then he returned to the abbey on Caldey Island. The current owner of this house knew Peter Anson and recalled that he had hundred's of books, but not much else (see photograph on page 28). He also remembers a framed certificate which took pride of place on a wall in the house. Peter told him he got it from the Pope. This must have been his certificate he received from Pope Paul VI, who made him a 'Knight of

## Nunraw Abbey (Sancta Maria Abbey)

The name Nunraw means 'Nuns row'. The present Abbey is built on the site of an ancient hill fort called White Castle, and sits at the foot of the Lammermuir Hills on the southern edge of East Lothian, approximately twenty miles east of Edinburgh. Today the Abbey is a working monastery, and was the first Cistercian house to be founded in Scotland since the Reformation (1560). The abbey was founded in 1946 by monks from Mount St. Joseph Abbey, Roscrea, Ireland, and was officially inaugurated as an Abbey in 1948. Grid Ref NT613686.

*Nunraw Abbey, East Lothian. (Renata Edge).*

Raymond Jaconelli is the current Abbot of Sancta Maria Abbey, he knew Peter Anson in 1975 when they were both at Nunraw Abbey, and Raymond confirmed that Peter moved to Nunraw from the remoteness of Caldey Island due to his poor health.

## Pluscarden Abbey

Pluscarden Priory in Moray lies in a broad glen known in former times as the 'Vale of St Andrew'. It was founded in 1230 by King Alexander II and remained as a priory until 1974 when its status was raised to an Abbey. During his time in the north east of Scotland Peter is known to have visited Pluscarden many times. In 1948 he wrote a book about the Abbey titled 'A Monastery in Moray'. Then in 1959 Peter republished this book after updating and expanding it.

*Pluscarden Abbey. (S. Bruce).*

Pluscarden Abbey has other connections with Banff and Macduff through the Duff family Earls Fife. In 1722 William Duff (1697 to 1763) later the 1st Earl Fife bought the Pluscarden Estate. James Duff (*1776 to 1857*) 4th Earl Fife in 1821 built the lodge, gates and gardens, and carried out many improvements to the Pluscarden estate particularly in the advancement of agriculture of which he is known to have been an enthusiastic pioneer. The estate remained in the Duff family until 1897 when Alexander Duff (*1849 to 1912*) the 1st Duke of Fife sold it to John Patrick Crichton-Stuart (1847 to 1900) the 3rd Marquess of Bute.

Pluscarden was raised to the status of an Abbey a year prior to Peter's death, and we can be sure that he would have been very happy about this. Grid Ref NJ142576.

## Tynet Chapel (St Ninian's)

Peter Anson wrote a piece about Tynet Chapel titled 'The Banffshire Bethlehem – St. Ninian's, Tynet – Scotland's Oldest Post-Reformation Catholic Church'. This was the first Catholic Chapel built in Scotland after the reformation of 1560. Tynet Chapel sits in a secluded spot off the A98 approximately half way between Buckie and Fochabers. (Grid Ref NJ378613).

This is a most unusual chapel, it looks like a plain harled cottage, and it's easy to pass it by without realising it is in fact a chapel. Peter wrote "There is nothing 'ecclesiastical' in its outward appearance." This was however part of its value to practising Catholics of the time because from 1725 to 1829 Catholicism was banned in Scotland. In 1725 Catholics were deprived of the use of the chapel at St Ninian's which was sited about one mile to the south east of Tynet. So from 1725 Catholics are thought to have gathered for mass in a barn provided by the laird Mr Gordon, with the minister disguised as a farmer. However after Culloden in 1746 this barn like many other chapels was burned to the ground by English soldiers. It wasn't until 1755 that the laird built the building which became Tynet Chapel as a sheepcote with a thatched roof as an extension to an existing cottage. This sheepcote was in effect built as a disguised chapel, and was used a safe place for Catholics to worship. It wasn't however until 1787 that the chapel took the shape we see today, at that time the chapel was again extended and slates from the old chapel of St Ninian's were used to roof most of it, the rest of it being slated in 1803. After its extension it was referred to as the 'Long Chapel', it is 121 feet long by 20 feet wide.

Peter also wrote "To the impartial student of Scottish history this humble chapel at Tynet has much in common with the graves of the

Covenanters, both reminding us of the age of religious persecution which, thank God, has now passed, at least in Scotland."

The chapel was restored in 1951 by Ian Gordon Lindsay and Partners of East Lothian.

*Tynet Chapel (St Ninian's), near Buckie. (S. Bruce).*

*Inside Tynet Chapel. (S. Bruce).*

*Tynet Chapel Alter. (S. Bruce).*

## St Ninian's Cemetery

This unusual November study reproduced in The Universe in 1938 was taken at St. Ninian's Cemetery, Banffshire, in the Catholic heartland of north east Scotland, of which the caption says: "In the past gave eight bishops and nearly 100 priests to the Church. Here are buried Bishop Thomas Nicholson, first Vicar Apostolic of Scotland, who died in 1719, also twenty-six other priests whose names are recorded on the cross in the centre of the picture (and also below). Close by is Tynet Chapel, the oldest post-Reformation church in Scotland." The figure in the picture is Peter Anson, at the time known as The Universe newspaper's 'Pilgrim Artist'.

*Peter Anson at St Ninian's, Buckie 1938. Courtesy J. Kelly, Editor of The Universe newspaper.*

*Cross at St Ninian's. (S. Bruce).*

*1687 carved stone, St Ninian's. (S. Bruce).*

**Lifetime Achievements (Summary)**

Peter wrote forty-seven books, and illustrated four others.

Peter drew thousands of paintings and drawings.

1921 - Peter co-founded the Apostleship of the Sea.

1922 - Peter was awarded with approbation of Pope Pius XI for his work of the Apostleship of the Sea.

1929 to 1936 - Peter had over eight hundred drawings published in 'The Universe' newspaper.

1936 - Peter was a founder member of the Society of Marine Artist's. (In 1966 it was renamed the Royal Society of Marine Artist's).

1966 - Pope Paul VI made Peter a 'Knight of the Order of St. Gregory'.

1967 - Peter was the first Curator of the Scottish Fisheries Museum in Anstruther, Fife.

*Peter Anson from the cover of his book titled 'A Roving Recluse' published 1946.*

**Timeline of Peter Anson's Life**

1889  22nd August – Frederick Charles Anson (Peter from *1924*) was born in the seaside resort of Southsea in Portsmouth.

1893  Peter's sister Edith Anson was born.

1894  Peter's sister Rachel Anson was born.

1898  Summer – Peter attended 'Little Appley' a small preparatory School in Ryde, Isle of Wight.

1901  Peter's father Charles Anson was awarded a CB, Companion of the Order of the Bath. *(Interestingly Prince Arthur of Connaught who married Princess Alexandra, Duchess of Fife (1891 to 1959) was awarded this honour in 1915).*

1902  Peter attended Wixenford boarding school, Wokingham (Founded in 1892) which at the time was one of the most expensive preparatory schools in England.

1903  Peter's brother Horatio Saint George Anson was born.

1904  Peter left Wixenford School Wokingham, just before his 15th birthday.

1905  Peter's Scottish born mother Maria Evelyn Anson (b.c1863 nee Ross) died. She was born on the Isle of Mull, on the west coast of Scotland.

1908 to 1910  Peter attended the Architectural Association School of London. He completed the first two years of a three year course before deciding it wasn't for him.

1909  30th April – Peter was confirmed as a member of the Architectural Association (AA) at an Ordinary General Meeting, he was proposed by Alan Potter and H.L. Samson. His address at this point was given as 102 Adelaide Rd., NW London. In his second year at the AA he is recorded in the register with the address of 22 Great College St. SW London.

1910  At the age of 21, Peter gave up his studies at the Architectural Association School in London. He then during April spent a two week trial at the abbey on Caldey Island off the coast of Wales near Tenby. Peter on the 31st July then joined the Anglican Benedictine Community at Caldey Island.

1913  Peter was received into the Roman Catholic Church.

1914  19th October – Peter due to ill health wasn't allowed to take his

Catholic vows alongside the other twelve monks who had come through their novitiate with him.

1915   September – Due to continued ill health Peter moved from Caldey Island and went to live in Portsmouth.

1915   December – Peter moved to Farnborough Abbey, where he stayed for three months.

1916   Spring – Peter's health improved and he returned to the Abbey on Caldey Island, where he stayed for ten weeks.

1916   Peter moved to Portsmouth to live with his grand-mother at 39 South Parade, Southsea, only a few yards from his place of birth. He stayed there for four months.

1916   September – Peter joined the Jesuits at Manresa House, Roehampton. Peter wrote "The spiritual exercises of St Ignatius churned me up inside and had precisely the opposite effect to what I had expected". Peter then appealed to the Abbot of Caldey Island to take him back, and once more returned to the abbey on Caldey Island.

1917   The work for Catholic Blue-jackets (WCB) passed to Peter who was a Benedictine oblate at the time. This organisation became the Apostleship of the Sea in *1921*.

1919   Peter's father Charles Anson was awarded a MVO, Member Royal Victorian Order. This order was created by Queen Victoria on the 21ˢᵗ April 1896. The order recognised those who had served the monarch with distinction. The order

*MVO Grand Cross. (Robert Prummel).*

had five grades, of which the Grand Cross was the highest grade, and Member the lowest.

1919   Peter had his first association with literature when his illustrations were used in a book titled 'Medley of Memories: Recollections of a Benedictine Monk', by Sir D. Hunter-Blair.

1919    December – Peter stayed for a while at Fort Augustus Abbey, Scotland. His mother had taken him to Fort Augustus when he was a wee boy.

1920    Peter spent the summer at Fort Augustus Abbey, and from here visited the Moray Firth coast. Peter was to return to Fort Augustus many times during his life.

1921    Peter co-founded the Apostleship of the Sea, which is an organisation dedicated to administering to the material and spiritual needs of Catholic sea-farers. Peter acted as the Honorary Organising Secretary.

1922    Peter travelled to Rome for the first time. He spent two months there, and was awarded with the approbation of Pope Pius XI for his work of the Apostleship of the Sea.

1922    Peter spent time at Fort Augustus, and on the Moray Firth in Scotland.

1922    March - Peter held his first exhibition of his work in Herbert Furst's Little Art Rooms in the Adelphi. The exhibition consisted of mainly marine drawings and water-colour paintings, many depicting the harbours of the Moray Firth.

1923    September – Peter spent time at Quarr Abbey, Isle of Wight.

1924    March – Peter resigned as Secretary of the Apostleship of the Sea due to ill health.

1924    2nd October – In Italy, Peter was admitted to the Third Order of St Francis, and he took the brown scapular. It was at this time that he took the name of Peter.

1925    Peter left the monastic community at Caldey Island.

1926    Peter spent several months in British Columbia.

1927    Peter returned to the UK, and established a studio in Portsmouth.

1927    Peter wrote his first book – 'The Pilgrim's Guide to Franciscan Italy'.

1929    Peter got a job with 'The Universe' newspaper and travelled throughout Europe making drawings of churches and abbey's which were reproduced each week in the paper. He became known as the 'Pilgrim Artist' and had over eight hundred drawings published. He continued this work until 1936.

1930    Autumn – Peter lived on the banks of the lower Thames first at Gravesend then at North-Fleet. He established a base here so he could be close to the publishing companies in London. He lived here until the Spring of 1934.

1933    Peter bought a horse-drawn gypsy caravan, and advertised for a travelling companion in 'The Universe' newspaper, and his advert was replied to by no less than 160 applicants, however it was Anthony Rowe who got the job. This journey was detailed in the book 'The Brown Caravan' written by Anthony Rowe published in 1935, and 'The Caravan Pilgrim' by Peter published in 1938.

1936    Spring - Peter spent two weeks on Barra, and then two months at Fort Augustus, before moving to Portsoy.

1936    Peter was a founder member of the Society of Marine Artists.

1936    May – Peter moved to a fisherman's cottage in Portsoy.

1936    December - Peter moved to two unfurnished rooms at Braeheads Banff, where he stayed for two years. Here Peter could look over Banff Bay and Banff Harbour.

1938    Peter ceased to take part in the affairs of the Apostolate of the Sea, but still remained a nominal member of its international council.

1938    May – Peter moved from Braeheads, Banff to No. 2 Low Shore, a small cottage aside Macduff Harbour known as 'Harbour Head'. He stayed in this house until 1952.

1940    Peter's father Charles Eustace Anson (b.1858) died.

1940    Summer - Peter and young Campbell Cowie from Macduff spent two weeks on the island of Iona.

1948    Peter acted as a representative for the Irish Government when they had some fishing boats built at Banff. Their new boat was called 'Rosa Mystica', and was blessed in Banff Harbour by Fr William Davis. Local shipwrights had never seen a Catholic priest muttering incantations in Latin out of a 'wee bookie' making signs of the cross and sprinkling the boat with water from a "wee bottlie". Three or four more boats were blessed, for the benefit of their Catholic crews.

1949    30th August - Peter's boat BF75 the 'Stella Maris' was broken-up due to old age, a brief entry in Peter's diary, states: "Alex John, Charley McKay, and self broke up Stella Maris". Most of the timber was burned, and "went up the lum". Breaking up of the Stella Maris Peter said "was the first step in the gradual breaking up of his own life".

1952 Peter sold Harbour Head, and moved from Macduff to the south of England. Seven months later – Peter returned to stay in Macduff, again he lived in a fisherman's cottage in Low Shore, sited to the east of Harbour Head. It is thought he regretted selling Harbour Head. (Both houses are now demolished).

*An early drawing of Harbour Head, Macduff, taken from Peter's book 'A Roving Recluse'. (Dated 1939).*

1958 Peter moved from Macduff to a cottage near Ramsgate Abbey.

1960 Peter moved from a cottage near Ramsgate Abbey to Park House B+B, Haywood Drive, Portsoy.

1960 Around September - Peter moved to Montrose and shared a twelve-room house with his good friend Jack Smith, which Jack had inherited from his parents.

1961 26th December – Jack Smith bought a large fisherman's cottage No. 17 William Street, Ferryden, near Montrose and Peter moved with him.

1962 July – Jack Smith got married so Peter moved to an unfurnished attic at No. 19 King Street, Ferryden, in the home of Andrew Mearns the local pilot and skipper of the 'Angus Rose'.

1963 February – Peter purchased No. 1 King Street, Ferryden.

1963    1st May - Peter moved into No. 1 King Street, Ferryden.

1966    Peter was honoured by Pope Paul VI, who made him a 'Knight of the Order of St. Gregory'. This honour was given a tribute to his prolific literary and scholarly achievements.

1966    The Society of Marine Artists co-founded by Peter in 1936, was renamed the Royal Society of Marine Artist's.

1967    April - Peter was approached to take on the Curator's position at the new Scottish Fisheries Museum in Anstruther. 8th July Peter officially became the first Curator. A position he held until January 1968.

1968    January - Peter moved from Anstruther to No. 3 King Street, Ferryden, near Montrose.

1969    Peter moved from Ferryden back to the abbey on Caldey Island. However Robert O'Brien of Caldey Abbey, recalled that Peter made a visit to the north east of Scotland every year.

*Ferryden, by Peter Anson 1974. (Courtesy Graeme Smith).*

1973    Peter donated four hundred of his paintings to Buckie Town Council. These were specifically donated for display in the new Maritime Museum in the Buckie Town House, Cluny Square. He also donated paintings to the National Maritime Museum in Greenwich, and also to the Scottish Fisheries Museum in Anstruther.

1974    Peter's old cottage 'Harbour Head', No. 2 Low Shore, Macduff was demolished during harbour improvements.

1975    Peter moved to Nunraw Abbey.

1975    June – Peter donated a further sixteen of his water-colour paintings to the Buckie Town Council.

1975    10th July – Peter died in St. Raphael's Hospital in Edinburgh, and was buried alongside other monks in the private cemetery for deceased monks at Nunraw Abbey. See pages 32 and 33 for photographs of the abbey.

1979    Moray Council received on loan an additional 430 of Peter Anson's paintings. These were on loan from the Abbot of Sancta Maria Abbey, Nunraw, East Lothian, who was bequeathed the copyright of all Anson's works.

1983    As part of the bi-centenary celebrations of Macduff several of Peter Anson's paintings were exhibited.

1994    A new 'Anson Gallery' was created at the rear of the Buckie Library.

*Peter Anson in his monks scapular, early 1970's, 17 William Street, Ferryden. (Courtesy Graeme Smith).*

**Sculpture - Idea**

The idea of a sculpture started when Association chairman Stanley Bruce as part of his job as a surveyor with DNV visited Aberdeen Specialists Welding and Fabrication Services (ASWFS) Dyce, Aberdeen, to witness some welder qualifications. ASWFS have a machine which cuts steel by high-pressure water-jetting, this process allows steel to be cut with intricate detail, and because the process uses water to cut the steel gives no distortion to the steel as found with flame-cutting. At the time Stanley Bruce was the Vice-Chairman of the Aberdeenshire Towns Partnership (ATP) Economic Development and Strategy Group for Banff and Macduff; and at several meetings had listened to proposals to create a maritime garden at Crook o' Ness Street, Macduff. So Stanley asked Paul Whyte of ASWFS if it would be possible for a steam drifter shape to be cut free of charge for erection in the garden, and Paul said "Yes". Stanley's first thought was that it could be cut from stainless steel and screwed onto the wall behind the garden, as the BMHA's contribution. In 2006 Stanley had prepared four pages of information about Peter Anson, which were displayed in the Banffshire Maritime Heritage Association exhibition in Macduff alongside one of Peter's watercolours, which was on loan. It was found from this that a lot of people in Macduff and Banff had never heard of Peter Anson, which Stanley found surprising because Peter had lived in the area for twenty-four years from 1936 to 1960. So Stanley then thought how can we remedy this? Stanley had noted that several other nearby towns have steel sculptures e.g. Fraserburgh town centre has 'The Net', Inverurie has the 'Salmon', Fochabers also has a 'Salmon' at the east entrance to the town, Stonehaven has a 'Dolphin' sited near the sea, and Ellon has an 'Otter' on the roundabout on the west side of the bridge in the centre of town.

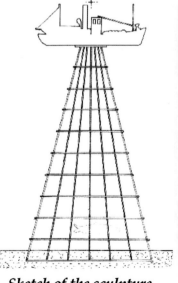

*Sketch of the sculpture. (S. Bruce).*

46

So if it was good enough for other towns its good enough for Macduff, and the idea of the net sculpture was born – Stanley sketched a four sided net under the proposed steam drifter based on the lines of the steam drifter BF251 'Loch Craig', and then added the herrings inside the net. The next problem was the cost, how can we pay for this? Then it was clear – each sponsor could have his name cut in a herring. Stanley then sketched a more detailed drawing to scale and reduced it from four sides to three, which reduced the amount of material needed but leaving it equally as strong.

## Sculpture – Artist's Impression

The artist's impression which was seen in the Press was prepared by Margaret McKenzie, Aberdeen, free of charge. Margaret is proficient in the use of Photo-shop and skilfully took Stanley's drawing and photographs to make the following impression. The anchor shown donated by DNV, Aberdeen, is currently in the safe hands of Aberdeenshire Council.

*Artist's impression of sculpture at Union Road, Macduff, by Margaret MacKenzie, Aberdeen.*

Stanley Bruce prepared a power-point presentation which was submitted to the Banff and Macduff Community Council back in September 2007. The proposal was agreed in principal subject to planning permission given by Aberdeenshire Council. The only comments given at the meeting were A) if it gets windy it could blow over. The sculpture will be bedded down with cement and there's no chance of it blowing over. B) It may get vandalised by children climbing up on it. The sketch showed the bars forming the net at 200mm spacing, this was changed to 100mm maximum spacing and these spaces reduce in width as you get nearer the top of the sculpture, so there is not a lot of space for a foot to fit in it. Then because the net mesh was made smaller there was a possibility of rubbish collecting inside the net so a change was made to lift the net clear of the ground, thereby giving access to underneath it for cleaning out.

## Sculpture - Construction

The net is the largest part of the sculpture and is made from solid round steel bars, 16mm diameter is used for the outer parts of the net and 12mm diameter for the rest of it. This net takes the form of a three sided pyramid with its centre slightly off centre to make it unsymmetrical, and a little more interesting. The focal point of the sculpture is the steam drifter which sits on top of the net. This part is also made of steel and was cut by high pressure water-jetting. Inside the net are herrings which are full size (300mm long). Each herring has a sponsors name cut in it. Under the steam drifter are three plates forming a triangle and these have had the following words cut in them again by the high pressure water-jetting process 'PETER ANSON', 'WRITER', and 'ARTIST'. The completed sculpture has been galvanised – this will prevent corrosion, and ensure it lasts for many years.

## Sculpture - Location

Today the sculpture is built, however its permanent home is still to be decided. According to the Aberdeenshire Council's guidelines for the erection of Public Art, there are procedures to be followed which include a public consultation, to get the views of the local community; this consultation will take place in Macduff Town Hall.

*Proposed sites so far are:*
  a) To the east of the petrol station, Union Road (As shown in the artists impression).
  b) Maritime Garden, Crook o' Ness Street.
  c) Near the Harbour Café (Appropriately where Peter's house 'Harbour Head' once stood.
  d) Piece of ground adjacent to the Waterfront Hotel, Union Road.
  e) At the east side of Banff Bridge.
  f) On a roundabout to be constructed in the new Industrial Estate.
  g) At the A947 entrance to Macduff adjacent to the cemetery wall.
  h) Anywhere else suggested at the public consultation.

**Sculpture – The Artist**
Stanley Bruce born in Fraserburgh in 1963, served his time as a Ship Draughtsman in Hall Russell, Shipbuilders and Engineers, Aberdeen. So he has had significant training in design work, he also worked in the yards management team in ship construction for over five years, so is aware of how to build using steel, however this is his first attempt at a sculpture. Stanley not only designed it but also cut the steel and fabricated it in his own free time, and with his own hands. Stanley has been the Chairman of the BM&HA since 2005, and also the Vice-Chairman of the Banff and Buchan Arts Forum from 2008 to 2009. Stanley stated "Should this be a success I have an idea for another interesting sculpture for Macduff" – so there may be more to come.

**Sculpture – Sponsors**
We are very thankful to the following sponsors who have contributed towards this project, without their assistance the project would never have been realised.

| Parts | Sponsor |
| --- | --- |
| Steel Rods | RDM Engineering, Turriff. |
| Drifter and cut lettering | DJR, Oldmeldrum. (Was ASWFS). |
| Herrings | Kelman Engineering Ltd, Turriff. |
| Welding assistance | ACE Winches, Banff. |
| Steel parts for the base. | A&B Welding, Aberdeen. |
| Galvanising | ACE Winches, Banff. |

| | |
|---|---|
| Information Panel | Still to be confirmed. |
| Booklet | Banffshire Maritime & Heritage Association. |
| Anchor | Donated by Det Norske Veritas (DNV) Aberdeen. |

## Sculpture - Completed.

The sculpture was completed in April 2009 by Stanley Bruce and fellow committee member Malcolm Smith of Banff, and was set up at the roadside (A947) at the premises of ACE Winches, Montbletton two mile south of Macduff. The sculpture has appeared in the Press and Journal, the Banffshire Journal, and has also been mentioned in the Tenby Observer in Wales.

*Stanley Bruce and the completed Peter Anson Sculpture (April 2009)*
*photo by Andrew Bruce.*

## Drift Net

The following drawings by Peter Anson show how a drift net was shot and how it floated in the water with buoys once shot. The herring were then caught by the gills in the mesh of the net. Peter's drawings have been added here to show that the net in the sculpture couldn't possibly depict this arrangement. Some herring drift nets were as long as two miles long. However if you look at the top drawing there is a triangular net shape which falls away from the boat when the net is being shot.

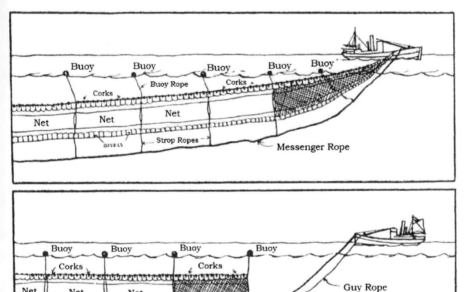

*Drift net being shot and in its final position.*
*Herring drift net by Peter Anson.*
*(Taken from Fishermen and Fishing Ways, published in 1932).*

The drift net was first successfully used in the UK in the 19th century; however drift net fishing became illegal in Scotland in 1962.

**Banff and Macduff Harbours Today**

In the Fishing Ports and Port Registration data recorded in 2003, BF (Banff, Scotland) is listed as "a tiny harbour, but registration port for many Scottish fishing boats. The adjacent port of Macduff is a major repair yard for fishing boats". Nine years into the new millennium there are approximately forty boats which still use Macduff as their home port. There is a thriving shipbuilding industry specialising in the construction of steel hulled fishing vessels and they still have the skills and capability to build a traditional wooden boat, although haven't now for a couple of years. In 2007 work began to enhance and redevelop Macduff slipway to make it safer and capable of taking the modern day boats which are larger and beamier and it now boasts a hydraulic winch and four vertical arm boat cradles, capable of lifting boats up to 550 tonnes. Some of Peter's paintings were made on the old slipway and he sure would have been interested in the modernisation if he'd still been with us.

Two years later, impressive new offices for Macduff Ship Design have been built behind the Harbour Café (Site of Peter's cottage – Harbour Head). Business is booming for Macduff in these days of economic recession, reflecting the words of George Scott-Moncrieff, who had observed in the economic downturn of the post-war years, that:

*Macduff Ship Design and the Harbour Café. (S. Bruce).*

"Macduff fishermen have established themselves as among the most go-ahead of all the communities".

Peter Anson's dedicated attention to detail has furnished us with a rich history of the fishing towns and villages of the north east of Scotland and beyond. "I never realised at the time", wrote Peter, "But the Moray Firth fishermen with whom I had been associating...diverted my whole life into new channels".

## Acknowledgements

Thanks to the following for their assistance in the publication of this book:

- Raymond Jaconelli, Abbot, Sancta Maria, Abbey, Nunraw, Haddington, East Lothian, for allowing us to reproduce some of Peter's work, and for many of the photographs in this book.
- Edward Bottoms, Architectural Association Archivist, 36 Bedford Square, London, for providing clippings from the Architectural Association Journals.
- Margaret MacKenzie, Aberdeen, for her artist's impression.
- Renata Edge for the two photographs of Nunraw Abbey.
- Raymond Vettese, Library Assistant, Montrose Library for information on Peter's time in Montrose and Ferryden.
- Wilma Woodin, Bookends, Portsoy for allowing us to use the photograph of Peter on the cover, and also for the photograph of the oratory in the loft of Harbour Head.
- The late Jim Gregor of Macduff who donated a copy of 'Fishing Boats and Fisher Folk on the East Coast of Scotland' which once belonged to his father, to the BM&HA in 2006.
- Deacon Brian Kilker, Aberdeen Port Chaplain of the Apostleship of the Sea for information on Peter and the AOS.
- Jim Aitken and the late Margaret Aitken, Cruden Bay, for information re the story of 'The Artist Monk of Macduff', published in 'Scottish Memories' September 2002.
- George Peattie, Ewan Cameron, Graeme and Anne Smith for their help and memories of Peter in Ferryden.
- John Aitken, Honorary Archivist Montrose Port Authority.
- John Woodside, Deacon, Our Lady of Mount Carmel Church, Banff.
- Robert O'Brien, Caldey Abbey, Tenby for his memories of Peter.

## Bookends Portsoy

This book shop at 21 Seafield Street, Portsoy has numerous rare copies of Peter's books. Go along and speak to Wilma if you'd like to purchase one. Tel 01261 842262.

## Appendix A
## Books written by Peter Anson
### 47 in total.

| Date | Title |
|------|-------|
| 1927 | The Pilgrim's Guide to Franciscan Italy. |
| 1930 | Fishing Boats and Fisher Folk on the East Coast of Scotland. (Republished 1971 and 1974). |
| 1932 | Fishermen and Fishing Ways. (Republished 1975). |
| 1932 | The Quest of Solitude. |
| 1931 | Mariners of Brittany. (Republished 1974). |
| 1934 | A Pilgrimage to Lourdes (Pilgrim's Sketch Books, no. 1). |
| 1934 | Forgotten Shrines of Britain (Pilgrim's Sketch Books, no. 2). |
| 1934 | A Pilgrimage to Brittany (Pilgrim's Sketch Books, no. 3). |
| 1934 | An Irish Pilgrimage (Pilgrim's Sketch Books, no. 4). |
| 1934 | A Pilgrimage in Italy (Pilgrim's Sketch Books, no. 5). |
| 1934 | A Pilgrimage to Liseux (Pilgrim's Sketch Books, no. 6). |
| 1934 | A Pilgrim Artist in Palestine. |
| 1937 | The Catholic Church in Modern Scotland 1560 to 1937. |
| 1938 | The Caravan Pilgrim. |
| 1939 | The Scottish Sea Fisheries – Are They Doomed? |
| 1940 | The Benedictines of Caldey. (Republished 1944). |
| 1941 | How to Draw Ships. (Republished 1942, 1943, 1944, 1947, and 2007). |
| 1944 | British Sea Fishermen. |
| 1944 | Harbour Head - Maritime Memories. (Republished 1945, and 2008). |
| 1946 | A Roving Recluse – More Memories. (Republished 2008). |
| 1946 | The Apostleship of The Sea in England and Wales. |
| 1946 | The Sea Apostolate in Ireland. |
| 1947 | Iona Abbey. |
| 1948 | Churches – Their Plan and Furnishing. (Republished 2007). |
| 1948 | The Story of Pluscarden Priory. |
| 1948 | The Church and the Sailor. |
| 1950 | The Religious Orders and Congregations of Great Britain and Ireland. |

**Appendix A continued**
**Books written by Peter Anson**
**47 in total.**

| 1951 | Welcome to the Deveron Vale: Banff and Macduff. |
|------|--------------------------------------------------|
| 1953 | Scots Fisher Folk. |
| 1954 | Christ and the Sailor. |
| 1953 | The Call of the Cloister. (Republished 1955, 1956, 1958, and 1964). |
| 1957 | These Made Peace (with Cecily Hallack). |
| 1958 | The Hermit of Cat Island. (Republished 1958). |
| 1958 | Abbot Extraordinary. |
| 1959 | A Monastery in Moray: the Story of Pluscarden Priory. (A rewritten and expanded version of his 1948 title). |
| 1960 | Fashions in Church Furnishings 1840 – 1940. (Republished 1965 and 1966). |
| 1960 | The Brothers of Braemore. |
| 1964 | Bishops at Large. (Republished 2006). |
| 1964 | The Call of the Desert. (Republished 1973). |
| 1964 | The Building of Churches. (Republished 1965). |
| 1964 | The Art of the Church. (Written with Iris Conlay). |
| 1965 | Fisher Folklore. |
| 1969 | Life on Low Shore. |
| 1970 | Underground Catholicism in Scotland 1622 – 1878. |
| 1971 | Fishing Boats and Fisher Folk on The East Coast of Scotland. |
| 1973 | Building up the Waste Places. |
| 1991 | The Sea Apostolate in the Port of London. (Published posthumously). |

**Appendix B**
**Books Illustrated by Peter Anson**
**4 in total.**

| 1919 | Medley of Memories by Sir D. Hunter-Blair. |
|------|--------------------------------------------|
| 1926 | An Old Story of a Highland Parish by George P. Shaw. |
| 1935 | The Brown Caravan by Anthony Rowe. |
| 1936 | A Last Medley of Memories by Sir D. Hunter-Blair. |

## Appendix C
## Peter Anson's Family Tree

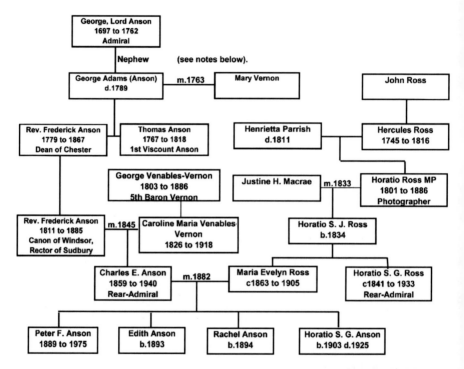

| | | | |
|---|---|---|---|
| **George, Lord Anson** 1697 to 1762 Admiral | | | |
| Nephew | (see notes below). | | |
| **George Adams (Anson)** d.1789 | m.1763 **Mary Vernon** | | **John Ross** |
| **Rev. Frederick Anson** 1779 to 1867 Dean of Chester | **Thomas Anson** 1767 to 1818 1st Viscount Anson | **Henrietta Parrish** d.1811 | **Hercules Ross** 1745 to 1816 |
| | **George Venables-Vernon** 1803 to 1886 5th Baron Vernon | **Justine H. Macrae** m.1833 | **Horatio Ross MP** 1801 to 1886 Photographer |
| **Rev. Frederick Anson** 1811 to 1885 Canon of Windsor, Rector of Sudbury | m.1845 **Caroline Maria Venables Vernon** 1826 to 1918 | **Horatio S. J. Ross** b.1834 | |
| | **Charles E. Anson** 1859 to 1940 Rear-Admiral | m.1882 **Maria Evelyn Ross** c1863 to 1905 | **Horatio S. G. Ross** c1841 to 1933 Rear-Admiral |
| **Peter F. Anson** 1889 to 1975 | **Edith Anson** b.1893 | **Rachel Anson** b.1894 | **Horatio S. G. Anson** b.1903 d.1925 |

Photograph shows a self-portrait of Horatio Ross, great-great-grandfather of Peter Anson, MP for Aberdeen and Montrose. Hercules Ross (1745 to 1816) was a great friend of Lord Horatio Nelson, and Lord Nelson was the Godfather of his son Horatio Ross (1801 to 1886). On the tree above you can see that four generations of Anson's from this family have taken the name Horatio after Lord Nelson. Peter had no children but left a legacy in his work.

*Horatio Ross. (1801 to 1886) A self-portrait c1850.*

## Appendix C (continued)

Peter's father Charles Eustace Anson (1858 to 1940) rose to the rank of Rear-Admiral, and served in the Navy for forty years. However in Harbour Head - Maritime Memories' Peter modestly tells that the only famous sailor amongst his ancestors is George, Lord Anson of Soberton (1697 to 1762) who received a peerage after a voyage around the world with a squadron of six ships of which 'HMS Centurion' was the flagship, and had many victories over the French and Spanish. George Anson served as the 'First Lord of the Admiralty' (1757 to 1762), and was referred to as 'The Father of the British Navy'. Peter also wrote that George Anson had no heir and his name, title and property went to his nephew George Adams (d. 1789) of Orgrave.

George Adams changed his name to Anson 30th April 1773, otherwise Peter would have been Peter Adams.

George Anson was MP for Hedon from 1744 to 1777. In George Anson's honour the Navy have named seven warships as 'HMS Anson' in his name as well as six others.

*Lord George Anson (1697 to 1762). (Artist unknown).*

## Appendix D
### Some of the boats Peter Anson records sailing on.

| | |
|---|---|
| BF75 Stella Maris | Peter's own small wooden hulled dipping lug fishing boat. He bought it in 1941, and it sank in 1952. |
| BF132 'Harvester' | As shown on the front cover of this book. |
| BCK381 'Monarch' | Wooden steam drifter built in Buckie in 1907 owned by Mr Clark. |
| SY26 'Perseverance' | 1950 – Built in Banff, owned by George Clark and Calum Morrison from the Isle of Bernera Outer Hebrides. |
| INS382 Brighton of the North' | 1921 - Nairn steam drifter. |
| BCK201 'Morning Star' | 1921 - Trawler, whose skipper was Peter Thain |
| ME34 'Rosemary' | 1960's - Ferryden fishing boat. |
| GY209 'Empyrean' | 1920 - He sailed to Grimsby. |
| 'Lady Agnes' | A Zulu sailing boat converted with an engine fitted, which Peter described as an "Evil smelling and dirty vessel". |
| 'Fiery Cross' | 1920 - Brixham Smack. |
| 'Nisha' | 1921 – A small beam trawler. |

Please note this is not a complete list, it's included here simply to show that Peter sailed with fishermen from many of the ports in the north east of Scotland.

### Another Interesting Read
Peter Anson - Monk, Writer, and Artist: An Introduction to His Life and Work (Paperback) by Michael Yelton (80 pages) published by the Anglo-Catholic History Society (Aug 2005) ISBN: 978-0955071409.

*Peter Anson at Macduff Harbour. (Courtesy Raymond Jaconelli).*

*Macduff Harbour, drawn by Peter Anson 1929.*

*Harbour Head, Macduff by Peter Anson.*
*(Peter's cottage is the one in the centre of the drawing).*

**Definitions (Encarta Dictionary).**
For those not familiar with the religious terms used in this book.

**Apostle** - any of the twelve followers of Jesus Christ chosen by him to preach the news about Christianity.
**Benedictine** - a member of a Christian order of monks and nuns founded by St Benedict of Nursia.
**Cistercian** - relating to an austere contemplative Christian order of monks and nuns founded by reformist Benedictines in 1098.
**Scapular** - a loose sleeveless garment worn by Christian monks, or two small pieces of cloth joined together and worn over the shoulder and back underneath other garments to signify membership in a Christian religious order or some other devotional purpose.

**Also:**
**Acromegaly** - overproduction of growth hormones, resulting in enlarged bones in the hands, feet, jaw, nose, and ribs of adults.